Travis D. Justus

Don't Know Much About Being a Leader in My Church

Don't Know Much About

Being a Leader in My Church

Douglas W. Johnson

ABINGDON PRESS
Nashville

DON'T KNOW MUCH ABOUT BEING A LEADER IN MY
CHURCH

Copyright © 1996 by Abingdon Press

All rights reserved.

This book is printed on recycled, acid-free paper.

Library of Congress Cataloging-in-Publication Data

Johnson, Douglas W., 1934–
    Don't know much about being a leader in my church / Douglas W. Johnson.
        p.   cm.
    ISBN 0-687-01706-8 (alk. paper)
    1. Christian leadership.   I. Title.
    BV652.1.64   1996
    253—dc20   96-4135
                                                                            CIP

96 97 98 99 00 01 02 03 04 05 — 10 9 8 7 6 5 4 3 2 1

MANUFACTURED IN THE UNITED STATES OF AMERICA

To the thousands of unheralded leaders who make
the world humane and special through their work in
the church

CONTENTS

Contents

How many times have you heard a plea like this one? "Leaders! I need leaders. I've had managers, counselors, and orators. But I need somebody who can create excitement in doing even the most drudge job, somebody who can melt the hardest heart, somebody who believes in the gospel so much that the Word becomes life, somebody who is scared to death to change but does it anyway, somebody who listens to an inner voice calling to a better way! I need leaders!"

And how many times have you responded, "Here am I, send me"?

Look at that response—uttered in the heat of the moment, in the unflagging belief that you can do something, in the commitment that you can change the world. But have you given any thought to the nitty-gritty questions such as how to become an effective leader in your church?

Your positive, hope-filled response needs to be nurtured. The leader in you is like an acorn that must be cultivated so that it sprouts and grows. The Word, the winds of turmoil, and the embrace of the church are critical if you are to grow into the leader God needs.

Perhaps you have books about leadership but found them focused on management or personal advancement or being an entrepreneur. Managing a mega-corporation, leading a team of scientists to harness the atom, or becoming a dictator are not our ideals of leaders for the church. And yet some of the characteristics of such leaders might also be found in that acorn of a leader within you. Give it a chance to grow and develop!

Some directions, proposals, and suggestions about nurturing the leader within you can be found in the following pages. Try them. Use the ones that work. Growing into a leader is a personal adventure that can be aided but never dictated by someone else's experiences.

"Who will go for me?" . . . "Here am I, send me!" Twenty centuries have not diminished the need, the thrill, or the difficulty of being a leader in the name of Christ.

What Do
I Do?

What do I do next? I have a manual with outlines, but am I supposed to do this by myself? Am I to do it any way I can?"

"Yes. You're in charge. The process is spelled out, and resources have been identified. It's up to you from this point on. The deadlines and expectations are clear. You have to work out everything so you can meet the expectations and deadlines."

This exchange took place in a regional planning meeting. The first speaker was groping for an affirmation of her responsibility as a leader. Her training and her service in local churches had not given her the leadership abilities she needed at this point. She had the *position* of leader, but she did not have an *understanding* that she was the leader.

Find Allies

If you want to be a good leader, the tools of leadership not only can be, but must be acquired. These tools deal with planning, delegating, supporting, directing, and acting. One such tool is finding and nurturing other leaders.

A member of one congregation was talking to a member of another church, sharing information about the clergy:

"Our new minister is O.K., I guess. He's not very smart when it comes to administration, especially in leading meetings. And he listens to the choir director too much. She's filling him full of gossip, and he's not paying attention to the real leaders of the church."

"I know what you mean. Our pastor has been with us for four years, and she still doesn't know who makes the decisions in the parish. She thinks a vote by the board is important! Things work in our church only if the small group of leaders, only one of whom is on the board, are behind them. So far, she's been lucky enough to try things they are behind. Only on a couple of occasions has the board voted for something and nothing has changed. Once was when she wanted to enlarge the nursery. The board voted for it, but the treasurers couldn't find the money and the banks didn't seem to want to lend us any. Of course, the real powers in the church were the treasurers, who also happened to be key executives in the banks."

"And she didn't know that?"

"No. I don't know what they teach ministers when they're in school, but somebody ought to clue them in on how the real world works."

There is a difference between elected or appointed leaders and real leaders. In many churches the real leaders are not elected leaders. How do you know the difference? Does a light suddenly shine or a neon sign switch on? To become a good leader, you need to learn how to work with other leaders. We will look at some ways to do that in the following chapter.

Beget Other Leaders

Good leaders want to help create new leaders—and they know how! They must allow the new leaders to carry out responsibilities and assume roles. Real leaders find ways to encourage and train others to become leaders. The problem that arises, of course, is that not everyone who is in a leadership position is comfortable with letting others take over a job.

"Our pastor seems to have an aversion to letting other people become leaders. He cannot accept the fact that growth in people as well as in the church occurs only when people are trained and allowed to function as leaders."

"That's strange. Doesn't he have any trust? Aren't ministers supposed to be in the business of helping people and churches grow? Why would he not let lay people be strong leaders?"

"I don't know. He's a nice man and I'm certain that if someone told him he was limiting growth of people and the church he would be very defensive and deny such a thing could happen when he was pastor. But the numbers tell the story!"

Leaders must learn how to trust and risk, otherwise they tend to revert to the common emotion of wanting to conserve and keep what they have. Protective and denying, they circle their wagons and blame outside forces for making change impossible.

About eight out of ten people are more interested in avoiding conflict and maintaining the status quo than they are desirous of change. The only way a leader can effectively initiate and promote change is to recognize this fact in herself or himself and in others, and then design strategies that will minimize conflict and enhance a situation so change and growth can happen.

People who prefer the status quo are fearful. They don't want to encounter the possibility that they might lose something. For example, it is not uncommon for persons who are living in intolerable situations to be afraid to change. It isn't that they don't want a better life. But they know their current boundaries, and these limits are preferable to the unknown.

Pastors and church members alike may find themselves in settings with little incentive—even though they espouse and support many ideas for change—to make the effort to lead for change.

Leaders Keep Learning
How to Lead

A third tool of leadership is continuous learning to be a leader. "What was good enough" then is not adequate now, nor will it suffice in the future. Effective leaders have to learn about themselves, about the people they are expected to lead, and how to adapt to change. This means their past experience will need to be used in new ways.

Testing and evaluating and sharpening your leadership skills are as necessary as a regular physical examination. A person does change; perceptions need to be tested and corrected; one church is not the same as others; people are not alike even though they may act alike; and words have different meanings when spoken by various groups and persons. None of these nuances of leadership change is even in the subconscious of leaders who are not testing themselves and learning new skills.

Leader—Manager—
Administrator

If you are going to be a good leader, you must be aware of various roles you must assume in differing situations. These roles can shift quickly at times so that you might have to act as a manager, administrator, and leader all within the course of one meeting.

Understanding the difference between leading, managing, and administering is crucial for leaders.

A leader's roles interact and overlap much like a moving collage. One role is management of the institution. A manager controls and directs the successful conduct of an institution. Such a person deals with educating, training, conducting, controlling, manipulating, and negotiating with many people in order to maintain an institution. Management is concerned with living within parameters of budget and procedures that he or she helped establish.

Administrating is a unique type of leadership. Mostly, administrators are dealing with rules and probabilities related to budget or activities within the organization that will keep it going. Administrators must use leadership skills.

A leader is one who guides, directs, and commands. In common situations this is the person who makes things happen, often where there are few resources and many naysayers. A leader is an entrepreneur, an individual who creates something out of nothing.

Leader—Manager— Administrator—Pastor

A fifth tool, one that applies especially to clergy, is understanding the role difference between being a pastor and leading.

For many clergy, being a pastor is a calling from God to be about the business of spiritual development in oneself and in those around. Humility and reflection are qualities often associated with this individual. Yet, people also expect the pastor to be manager, administrator, and leader of a local church. The pastor comes to these tasks with a wealth of training on introspection and how to do spiritual development.

Pastors are entrusted with a profound message of love and live with continual pulling from persons who need spiritual healing and spiritual fulfillment. Pastors have demands and pressures unlike those of other professionals. They are required to function as leaders in a variety of roles.

If you are a pastor, you know that pastors are people who bring to their jobs the same needs and hopes and gifts others bring to their tasks. The difference is that pastors are separated into a role of spiritual leadership. They lead the community to God's grace in moments of joy, sorrow, depression, and elation. The fact that a pastor can help individuals and families and inspire congregations suggests that this same individual, with help, can lead in planning, evangelism, stewardship, education, and administration in a church. But pastors need help with leadership training too.

Leadership—Learned or Innate?

While some leadership skills are innate, much can be learned and shaped to the needs of local churches or institutional leadership. This book assumes that appointed or elected leaders are willing to learn how to be real leaders. It is designed to awaken a response that allows appointed or elected leaders freedom and encouragement to take risks associated with becoming real leaders. It provides suggestions about being a leader that can make a difference in how you lead.

CHAPTER TWO

Spotting and Using Natural Leaders

We have established that leaders come in a variety of packages. As you are in the process of becoming an effective leader, in organizations and in churches, you will come across various natural leaders. How do you recognize them? A good way to begin is with observation of different types of natural leaders.

❖ ❖ ❖

The Talker

"Harry talks everything to death. He will argue during a meeting until the board or committee votes his way just to keep him quiet. But nothing ever happens after the vote."

"We have all kinds of psychological terms to describe him, but we need to do something so he doesn't wear people out by talking."

"Harry probably doesn't want to change; he likes the status quo and will attack any proposal that threatens his status or well-being. His attacks usually are oblique and somewhat off the point but cogent enough to redirect the group's thinking."

"Much of the time that's true. But once in a while he comes up with a pretty good idea. For example, the other night he suggested we begin looking at enlarging the building to accommodate some of the new people who are building homes and moving into the apartments within a mile of the church. That didn't sound like an attack."

"It is an oblique attack. Think about the effects of enlarging the building and getting new people. There would be no need to consider moving the church, another church wouldn't be started, a larger financial base would result which would make life somewhat easier, and the church Harry loves would be growing in size and influence in the community. Harry wouldn't have to change anything he holds dear by making that suggestion."

"But his church will change. It will become more diverse because of the ages of the newcomers. And the programs will change."

"Right. But look at it from Harry's point of view. He's getting older and has already had to adjust to younger voices, including those of his children. He can tolerate program adjustments because he doesn't have to be involved in a lot of programs—he can pick and choose. The big thing, though, is that Harry hasn't disturbed his church. It will continue as is into the future, and he had a voice in making that happen. He will still be a member of the top-status church in town."

The Talker is interested in keeping the status quo. This person is appealing since he or she is similar to the 80 percent of us who don't like change—who prefer the status quo because we fear the unknown and believe change will somehow diminish our well-being. For many of us, the word *change* is like waving a red flag at a bull. However, we *can* tolerate

    adjustments,

    enhancements,

    growth, and

    slight revisions, clarification, or improvements.

The subtlety of these words signifying change should not be lost on would-be leaders in churches and organizations. Change *is* possible for those who prefer the status quo, but such change must not be like a tidal wave. People must be allowed to consider, think about, and digest the implications of change before it can become palatable. They must also know the immediate effect of change on them and their sphere of influence before they will accept it.

If you work with Talkers you should know that Talkers can be good natural leaders at specific times after a bit of training. Before a new idea is presented to a Talker, it must be carefully thought out and implications of change for every segment of the congregation identified. Implications of a change must be stated in the most positive language possible so that negatives, while identified, are perceived as slight impediments that can be overcome.

Patience is required in working with Talkers, but they are powerful supporters when it becomes clear that no one is out to get them, ignore them, or discount their ideas. They need to be listened to for their message, not their verbiage.

Talkers' leadership style may appear to be negative and can become unpleasant if ignored, ridiculed, or allowed to continue unabated. However, you can use it as an early warning system to test ideas and to make certain that proposals for new programs or concepts can pass the scrutiny of many of the people in the congregation. Talkers are helpful, informal leaders if they are recruited to "pass the word" that the new idea will have positive effects on them and their friends.

For example, a congregation met in a very poor location, and someone suggested it might make sense to move it to a new place. This brought an immediate negative reaction from a group led by a Talker on the board. Several sessions of the board were held to carefully consider the current versus the proposed location. These sessions dealt with membership, programs, looking at where current members live, looking at several possible sites and the kinds of people moving into those areas, and the financial resources and needs such a move might require. At each of these meetings, the Talker brought the negative mirror to all of the proposals.

The leader, who happened to be the pastor, sensed the need of this person and others like her to maintain the status quo. In a private conversation, the pastor spent time with her to discuss her stake in the current building and program, her family's history there, and what it might mean to her to move. The discussion moved to how the history might be continued and enhanced by moving as opposed to closing down the church (which was a possibility within a decade). The pastor talked about how she might make the move an opportunity to enhance the church as a place in which her family's history might take on new depth through her giving a memorial to put into a new building.

After three such meetings between the pastor and the Talker, the mood in the meetings shifted to the need for relocation and a sort of impatience with continuing the discussion and not acting. The result was a vote with a large majority in favor and the Talker being the person making the motion to move.

The Talker had done what she had been entrusted to do—bring her influence to bear on her friends in the congregation so that they moved from opposers to supporters. The pastor recognized her importance as a natural leader and her opposition as a firm desire to maintain personal well-being and status. Most of her friends voted with her, and those who did not continued to be suspicious of the "smooth-talking pastor."

The Doer

Doers are a special breed. Give them an idea about something and all of a sudden, it's done. It is not uncommon for Doers to forget a few details, making their deeds semi-sweet.

"I'm afraid to tell Jimmy any of my new ideas. If I do and he likes it, chances are he'll try to get something going. A month ago, I mentioned that we probably needed to start a single-adult ministry. Within a week, Jimmy had announcements for a meeting all made and was posting them. Good thing I caught him at the start. He didn't have the foggiest if we had enough singles to make up a group, what kinds of programs might be appealing to them, the kinds of singles who might come, age differences, and other details of program planning. It could have been a disaster."

"That describes Elaine in our church. I suggested that the women's organization needed to start evening groups. Almost before I had it out of my mouth, Elaine had gathered half a dozen young women, set a date for a first meeting, and started designing a program. These were great steps except she didn't bother to contact anyone from the women's organization. Elaine doesn't like to sit in meetings and discuss things without taking action. Our problem, just like yours with Jimmy, is her acting without attention to detail."

Doers are aggressive. They want to see immediate results. They have good ideas and can get people to act because of their own enthusiasm. They make good sales contacts, but they need help in closing the deal because they don't like to handle details. In the best sense, they are the beginners, but someone else will be needed to be sure there is an end to the project.

"Joe is one of our best idea persons. He comes up with an idea and can outline what needs to be done and proceeds to work . . . up to a point. Then he seems to lose interest and must go on to the next project. We often are left with a bunch of projects that need to be completed. It gets pretty hairy sometimes."

A Doer is the kind of natural leader some churches need to get a jump start. A Doer has the idea and can move quickly. However, Doers should not be given an entire program or project without being teamed with people who handle details well. A Doer's attention span is limited, necessitating your energy and careful monitoring of the Doer's activity. If a Doer can be teamed with someone who is comfortable in making certain all the details are attended to, a Doer can be a godsend to a congregation.

Doers, unfortunately, are not leaders in whom people will place long-term commitment. After being disappointed with unfinished projects, followers will abandon Doers for other, more sedate and less exciting leader types. But Doers bring energy and enthusiasm to the church. They are an important part of the leadership once you discover and are able to use their unique capabilities and to team them with others who will complete programs and projects.

T-h-e P-r-o-c-r-a-s-t-i-n-a-t-o-r

Procrastinators will "get around to it" in the near or far term. In total, these persons kill more projects than any other kind of leader. Although procrastinators have great intentions, time never seems to be an element in their planning. But somehow Procrastinators often are able to pull off projects even if all the planning is not done well. They are marvels at getting it done just in time. They seem to thrive on the thrill of working under a great deal of pressure.

Procrastinators typically have many irons in the fires of whatever organization they are part of. They like to be active, and they like the attention they get for being active. They have good ideas and have the planning skills needed to make most projects run smoothly. Their primary difficulty is that they have so much to do, they forget, put things off, or rest at the wrong time, and find themselves in a pinch for time at inappropriate points in program or project development.

One congregation had a Procrastinator at the head of its long-range planning committee. This same individual was working full time, was a member of the boards of directors of five community organizations, and a consultant on time management. She led the church committee to the conclusion of its report, but the report was late and was not as helpful as it could have been in assisting the building committee in deliberations about the new facility it was planning.

This woman was overloaded. She had leadership skills. She fit the profile of a Procrastinator because she had so many other things in which she was interested that she was unable to prioritize her time to meet the deadlines of all of the groups to which she was responsible.

Procrastinators are important natural leaders in particular situations. They can pick up an organization whose leadership group is unwilling to try something new or to tackle a difficult problem. The Procrastinator will volunteer and begin some action even though others on the committee may say, "With this person in charge, nothing's going to get done."

It is at the second or third or fourth step in the project that time becomes a factor. Perhaps the energy level lowers dramatically or interest in the program has peaked and a new challenge has taken hold of the individual. Somewhere down the line, the Procrastinator will let deadlines slip past. At this point, as we have suggested with the Doer, another person may be teamed with the Procrastinator so that the project or program may continue to a successful conclusion.

As a real leader, you must be ready to keep track of the progress of the Procrastinator's effort. Providing a safety net by having someone else team with her or him at a critical time is very important.

These three types of persons are in every church's leadership cadre. They have important contributions to make as long as their strengths are emphasized as well as their weaknesses realized.

Think about natural leaders such as these as being like members of a symphony orchestra where each of the contributors is as important as the others. As in the orchestra, many leaders play their roles without being featured or headlined. Leaders do not have to be at the head of the charge up a hill. They can be the persons who talk a thing to death or do a half-baked job of something just to get things going or begin a project and then bog down somewhere along the way. Each has a piece of leadership that can be utilized and melded with the skills and aptitudes of others to make a successful church program.

You will be a much more effective leader if you are aware of the natural leaders you are likely to encounter and some specific ways in which you might relate to them.

A Word About Meetings

Meetings can remind you of watching the same movie over and over. You know the actors, anticipate their reactions, and can recite their lines for them. Yet meetings are the soil in which leadership is sprouted. Meetings are the channelers of action in an organization.

At a meeting, you are likely to discover Talkers, Doers, and Procrastinators sharing space in the same room. But there are others, too, who are equally important: Conciliators, Negotiators, Finishers, and Problem Solvers.

The Conciliat☺r

Conciliators bring about truces during debates and discussions. These individuals possess the ability to take over leadership at particular and crucial times in the life of a church or other organization—such as when aggressive and combative persons, charged by an issue or because of some physical or emotional problem, create unpleasant stalemates in organizational activity.

For example, when one organization had the opportunity to upgrade its telephone system, furious debate arose between two key individuals who were charged with making a decision about which company to use. After four futile meetings, a Conciliator took it upon himself to talk with both persons and help them find a common ground on which to proceed. The process took the Conciliator several days, but by the next committee meeting the impasse had been broken, the issue had been resolved, and a decision was possible.

A Conciliator is a leader with special skills that are most apparent at critical times of divisiveness. Conciliators bring to the table sympathy with the individuals involved, but they and often have no strong feelings (or at least downplay their emotions) about the issue under discussion. The Conciliator is a natural leader who can live his or her lifetime in a church without being recognized as crucial to its long-term success.

31

The Negotiator

Negotiators function in the midst of meetings, not behind the scenes as Conciliators often do. Negotiators are looked to for solutions that can be accepted by everyone during a discussion or debate. They help the group discover alternative ways to think, to develop programs, raise money, finance special projects, and initiate new activities. Negotiators find ways to get things done.

Negotiators can be trained somewhat, but their inner strengths are evident prior to training. They have egos strong enough to admit to being wrong, to withstand personal attacks, to endure periods of negative feedback, and grace to accept congratulations. Negotiators may not be evident on a committee or in a meeting until there is a problem. At that point they begin to help participants find ways to create a commonly acceptable alternative.

The Finisher

Finishers are detail oriented. They have a habit of saying "Yes, but . . ." They are not quick to endorse new ways of acting or grandiose plans. They are dealing with the "how's," "when's," and "why's" of issues while others are content to handle the "what" and "where." They come in to "mop up" situations more than to initiate. Finishers are a crucial additive to the work of Doers and Procrastinators.

Finishers revel in handling details. They ask the annoying questions that are essential to getting things done. The point of their questioning is to make certain that plans are executed. Their presence in a committee is important, but they should not be allowed to dominate since they sometimes come across as negative. This is not intentional; they merely want all the facts before letting a project proceed.

A Finisher's leadership ability is in the knack for seeing the total picture. Many people have no interest in "seeing the whole" in the same sense as the Finishers because their interest is in individual items rather than the total.

Finishers are frequently misunderstood because they can have trouble framing their questions in a positive and supportive manner; sometimes they are viewed as promoting the status quo.

While the contributions of Finishers may seem to be moving against a positive future, careful analysis of their point of view can lead to new and better ways of handling situations or program issues. Finishers can be a tremendous help because they raise the questions that need to be answered before the start of a building program, an expanded program for a particular age group, or a new church or church-school class. Their penchant for detail must be part of any discussion, even if the issue being discussed is creating a vision for the future.

The Problem Solver

Problem Solvers may come in the shape of Conciliators, Finishers, Talkers, Doers, or Negotiators. Problem Solvers are persons who can quickly think through issues and help a committee or another leader follow through on a plan. Their contributions seem so obvious to them that Problem Solvers often feel they are not important.

Problem Solvers are prevalent in congregations and organizations but often are overlooked or ignored because they may be overpowered by a Talker or put off by a Procrastinator. These persons are not leaders in the traditional sense because they often are not put in positions of visibility or power. Yet, they naturally perform leadership functions as truly as do those who have the official stamp of leadership.

Informal Meetings

The best way you can discover and encourage others in their own leadership capacities is to meet them in informal settings. They feel more comfortable in non-formal situations because the context of the meeting is less likely to be combative or stressful. Some natural leaders like their anonymity within the structures but are quite aware of their abilities to sway discussions. They need to be listened to and supported.

Some of the most successful real leaders put together small groups of natural leaders, often taking persons with skills described above to help chart a plan, to receive feedback, to test ideas, and to receive a quick reading of the current pulse of the congregation. You should try to schedule such a meeting so the atmosphere is cordial and friendly—perhaps during a meal. You might not want to take minutes of an informal meeting, but you should write down ideas that might be forgotten later. These informal meetings allow each type of leader to participate and to learn from one another. In one sense, you are acting as a leader and are being kept informed, but a second effect is interchange and learning by all participants.

Informal meetings offer opportunities to learn about the aptitudes and skills of others. Without such informal settings, those in charge of churches and organizations are at a disadvantage in utilizing the skills of the natural leaders in their midst.

Private Conversations

Private conversations tend to be overused by organizational leaders, and you should be judicious about employing them. While you might consider them informal and non-threatening, people with whom you are talking might construe them as stressful. This is especially the case if you are new in your leadership position. For those who have built a reputation within the church or organization, conversations with you may be considered to be subversive.

Conversations may test ideas and feelings, but these are better done in a small group where people are comfortable with one another. Trust is built not in private but in public activities. Good leaders do not rely on information taken in private because it may not be accurate, acceptable to reveal, or helpful to the person who gave it. Private conversations are viewed by many as confidential sharing that should not be made public.

Being a leader in your church is like living in an eggshell. The eggshell can be shattered by many different sources. But on the positive side, the eggshell can break because something is being born of your leadership.

CHAPTER THREE

Characteristics of Effective Leaders

Each leader brings strengths to a task. A true leader is able to recognize her or his strengths as well as the best leadership traits of others. Therefore, one of the most important characteristics of a leader in a church organization is *knowing your own strengths*.

Know Your Strengths

This knowledge is not as easy to acquire as you might be led to believe. Self-administered instruments abound for discovering your leadership strengths and aptitudes. The caution in relying on such instruments and their resulting categorizations is that within each of us lie most of the traits we need to be good leaders. The predominance of one or two traits does not mean we lack others. Such tests tend

Ten Characteristics of Effective Leaders

1. Know Your Strengths

2. Recognize the Leader in Others

3. Be Willing to Listen

4. Be Willing to Incorporate New Ideas

5. Keep Your Purpose Before You

6. See and Communicate Your Vision

7. Deal Constructively with Conflict

8. Be Patient

9. Be Empathetic

10. Be Dependable

to categorize leaders rather than allowing them to see areas of dominance along with traits that can be developed. You can develop your less dominant traits if you want to do so.

Recognize the Leader in Others

The second trait of a good leader is *recognizing and capitalizing on the leadership capabilities of others.* Many would call this the ability to delegate. In the church, delegation of duties and powers is done differently than in business or other organizations. Work in the church is accomplished by *empowering* others. Empowerment is a supportive process that includes allowing people to use their leadership in a variety of activities. Empowerment demands time and energy by a leader to ensure that the individual who has been given a role has the tools, understands time and budget limitations, and knows to whom he or she is responsible. Empowerment allows the individual to do the job in whatever way seems comfortable and appropriate.

Some leaders are defensive about recognizing others' capabilities. But strong leaders surround themselves with capable colleagues, some of whom surpass the leader in certain areas of expertise. These colleagues will provide opportunities for the leader to grow, and can help generate innovative ideas and ways of doing things.

This second characteristic must include *utilization* as a key phrase. It is not enough to *recognize* other people's capabilities. A good leader helps place other good leaders in situations that will produce effective programs. A leader who is afraid someone else will do a better job than he or she does needs to understand that no leader can alone do the tasks necessary to make a church more effective.

Be Willing to Listen

The third characteristic of an effective leader is *willingness to listen*. It's fine, even necessary, to have a strategy and an item-by-item plan. But the plan will be impossible to implement unless others are willing to help. Their willingness to help is directly correlated to the leader's willingness to listen and amend plans when appropriate.

How can a leader know what the followers will agree to support unless she or he hears what they are saying? Hearing involves not only understanding the words but also *respect* for the speaker. In this sense, being willing to *listen* means hearing and heeding what is being uttered.

Be Willing to Incorporate
New Ideas

The fourth characteristic of an effective leader is *willingness to incorporate other people's ideas* into proposed programs or actions. Every idea, of course, will not be useful or practical. People often present ideas to test the ability of a leader to maintain composure and to stick to a plan. Such testing will appear to be quite legitimate, and suggestions must be taken seriously. Careful thought and consideration about all aspects of a proposal may result in a new way of looking at a program and a different plan than had been proposed.

Some people call the incorporation of other people's ideas into a leader's plan a negotiated plan, but this is not necessarily the case. A wise leader knows one person cannot anticipate as many opportunities and problems with a proposal as can a small group of people. For this reason, leadership is shared with a team, whether among a church staff or among volunteers.

For every dark cloud there is sunshine and for every raindrop there is a rainbow. An individual may not be able to see beyond the clouds and the rain while others on the team can help find the beams and the colorful promise of new opportunities. Listening and using other people's ideas to strengthen and broaden programs are key traits of an effective leader.

Keep Your Purpose
Before You

The fifth characteristic is the ability to *help others be continually aware of the purpose of their activity.* The purpose of the church and its organizations is to spread the gospel of God's love as proclaimed in the life of Jesus

Christ. The process of spreading this gospel takes many forms, but prior to initiating any program it is essential to test it with the purpose of the church.

There are legitimate differences of opinion about the means of proclaiming the gospel. Some believe the emphasis should be on equality of treatment for all people. Some adhere to the belief that God has chosen certain groups and certain people to be the primary examples of the message. Some think they may use any force against others that they wish because they alone have the truth. The means must be tested by the purpose. It is the leader's task to make certain this test is given to each proposal made in the name of the church.

The relocation of a church or the merger of two congregations are strategic possibilities related to resources. They may also have a bearing on the purpose of the church. If the relocated church can be more effective in proclaiming the gospel, or if the union of two churches into one will produce strengthened witnessing, the purpose of the church becomes an important overall consideration. How the question is raised in either instance leads us to the sixth characteristic of an effective leader.

See and Communicate Your Vision

The sixth characteristic of an effective leader is *seeing and communicating a workable vision* for the church and its organizations. Notice the need not only to see the vision yourself but also to communicate this vision so others will believe it to be workable and own it with you. Being esoteric and philosophical has a place, but this place is not with a leader who is attempting to mobilize people to initiate and support programs of outreach and ministry for the church.

If you are able to use language that grabs the attention and catches the heart and imagination of hearers, you will be able to convey a vision that raises sights, ignites hopes, and seems within the range of possibility. Such language is the gift and trait of an effective leader.

I know a young man who has a limited mental capacity that causes him to be repetitive and slow of speech. This same young man can describe a scene from a James Bond movie in a flawless, animated narrative that changes voices with the introduction of different characters. He is transported beyond himself through the movie. Isn't this a metaphor for a leader in the church? Many people in the church want to be transported into another relationship that allows them to understand the emotion and depth of God's love. The creation and communication of such a vision is a trait of an effective leader.

Deal Constructively with Conflict

The seventh trait of an effective leader is the *ability to deal constructively with conflict*. Conflict resolution is hard for those who have been taught to turn the other cheek, to forgive, and to love in spite of rancor. Nevertheless, conflict is a part of life, a good part of life.

Conflict can be channeled into constructive paths in many situations. In most cases, conflict tests your resolve and faith. Arguments over money or status are not worthy to be called conflicts. They are petty disagreements regardless of the amount of money or the height of status. Conflict occurs when there is a serious question about purpose, ethics, or character. Deciding whether to remain faithful, and struggling with a decision about the direction of your life are legitimate arenas of conflict.

Conflicts in the church are more humdrum. They occur because one child rather than another is chosen for a leading part in the youth play, someone else is selected to be the chairperson of a prestigious committee, or the preacher's sermon unfairly criticized a particular group. These are the types of conflicts, multiplied a thousandfold by others even less dignified, that bedevil church leaders.

The best method for dealing with conflict is going to the source of the problem and hearing a clear statement of the grievance. Once this is done, you may be able to use other leadership characteristics to bring the person back onto the team as a productive member. On the other hand, not talking to the problem maker and allowing others to intervene and carry messages will aggravate the problem and alienate the agitator.

Other methods for handling conflict include using a mediator (when the problem is immense or no face-to-face resolution is possible), apologizing and working out an agreeable solution as well as seeking to avoid further slights or injury, or, in some situations, declaring that the best resolution of a conflict is to agree to disagree and try to keep to other topics when you must face the aggrieved individual. A different solution is for one or the other of you to go to another church and not bring up the past.

Be Patient

An eighth characteristic of an effective leader is *patience*. Human endeavors take time. My thinking and emotional processes may take more time to adjust than yours. Give me time to get adjusted to your idea or proposal; don't make me decide this minute. But give me a deadline because if you don't, I might not be ready to think about it again.

Remember, eight out of ten of us like to keep things as they are; we don't relish change. Allow us time to help create the strategy, the plan, the program, and we'll come around. Push us too fast and you've lost us. Show us how the changes will benefit us and those we hold dear. If you can do that, we will eventually think you are phenomenal.

Patience is a virtue to be nourished. It is not inborn. Learn to put a trap on your tongue. Remember to listen to the content of the words of others. Learn to wait a while before expressing your opinion or a criticism of another person's idea or position. Notice that when you make an issue of something, you cause others to defend the other side even though they may not want to be in that position. Consider other people's feelings before you speak or act.

Be Empathetic

A ninth characteristic of an effective leader is the ability to *empathize*. Wearing the other person's shoes for a while can cool our criticism. Effective leaders cultivate the ability to "see" the world as does someone who is unable to see or "listen" like someone who cannot hear or wonder at everything like a child. None of us is all-knowing or all-seeing. We need to feel what others feel.

A lesson you can learn by exposing yourself to as many other cultures as you can is the variety of truth that experiences generate. A dirty hovel in the mountains of one nation may be luxury to a street dweller in a squalid slum in another country; but in both settings, life begins and ends, ethics are taught, love is practiced, and God is venerated. People are bound by the heart—by a mother's love, a child's dependence, a desire to be better, to do more, to be recognized—more than they are bound by the external situations in which they live. A leader understands this and practices the ability to share experiences with others without having to share their exact life-style.

Be Dependable

A tenth characteristic of an effective leader is *to be dependable*. If you say you are going to do something or be somewhere, do it and be there. If you know you can't hold up your end of a promise, don't make it. You can be an exciting and out-front leader. Dependability is living out what you promise to do.

This list of ten characteristics does not exhaust the skills needed, nor is it a complete catalogue of leadership traits you have in you. However, these ten characteristics are crucial to those who work with people in the church and other settings dependent on volunteers. They are characteristics most needed in dealing with people who are peers, who can leave the church without penalty, or who can be recruited and excited by opportunities for service.

Wrap these ten characteristics together and you will be a leader of much potential. Infused with the Spirit of Christ, you will act with thoughtfulness, care, and respect for others.

Don't let the desire to be "loving" and "pastoral" overshadow your leadership characteristics. A pastor leads and manages and administers in a church; the roles shift constantly. As you learn more about being a leader, you will shift intentionally at times, especially when you are faced with hard decisions. You will find yourself relying on other people's ideas and skills instead of insisting on having your way, and you will surely deal with conflict.

47

These times will test your commitment to being a leader. It takes as much courage to be a leader as it does to be a pastor. The rewards are the same— growth in people and a vibrant institution. Keeping the rewards in mind is essential as we discuss risk taking.

CHAPTER FOUR

Risk Taking as a Leadership Role

We never seem to be at a loss for opportunities to take risks. Being a *good* leader requires taking at least the following four risks.

Risk 1: Learning New Things

A consultant was invited to visit a church that felt it needed to make changes in its programs. He suggested that the church provide better lighting throughout the building; print more bulletins in order to accommodate more visitors; set up procedures for contacting members who have not attended church during the past two weeks; put up signs so people know where to go for classes, the office, and restrooms; and start and end the worship service on time.

Risk Taking
as a
Leadership Role

Risk 1. Learning New Things

Risk 2. Learning About Yourself

Risk 3. Trusting Others

Risk 4. Training Others

Three months later, this same consultant visited the church and discovered that nothing had changed. He was not surprised because his sessions with the pastor and the board confirmed that the leaders of this church were comfortable with the status quo. They talked about change but were unwilling to risk making any efforts to change.

A pastor went to a workshop on worship. She learned new ways of doing services, innovations in the liturgies, tips on beautifying and improving the atmosphere of worship, and suggestions on training ushers. She returned home with a list of proposed changes in her church and a schedule for implementing those changes.

She met with a small group of leaders and proposed changes in the sanctuary that would improve its appearance. She took the leaders into the sanctuary and pointed out the areas where change would enhance worship. The leaders raised questions and gave counter suggestions. They all agreed to think about the proposals and possible revisions for a week.

The next week the pastor met with the leaders again and told them her new thinking, based on results from the previous meeting, and asked for their thoughts and suggestions. One of the leaders asked that they go into the sanctuary because he had an idea. In the sanctuary, he explained what he had in mind and proposed a plan for getting it done. The rest of the group endorsed the proposal and agreed to bring it to the congregation during the worship service two weeks hence.

In preparation for that service, the pastor and the lay leader of the congregation sent a brief letter to the membership explaining what was to be proposed. In order to make certain as many people were aware of the plan as possible, the letter was included as an insert in the worship bulletin the next two Sundays.

At the worship service on the day of the congregational meeting, the pastor explained why she had begun making slight changes in the worship service such as starting the service on time, shortening the sermon and keeping to the point, having a single theme for the service, allowing less time for verbal announcements and giving more details in the bulletin, and increasing the number of printed bulletins. She then introduced the lay leader, who presented the proposal for improving the appearance of the sanctuary. After the presentation there was a question-and-answer session, followed by a vote by the congregation on the improvements. The person who had made the original suggestions for sanctuary improvements stood after the vote and made a verbal pledge of several hundred dollars as a start on the project.

The pastor's handling of this episode in the congregation's life demonstrates risk taking for a leader. First, she took a risk by going to the workshop. This step was not an easy one. She had to decide that she was willing to test her worship style against others. She might have been motivated by a conviction that she had an adequate style for the congregation's worship service, a desire to show others how innovative and creative she was, a feeling that something needed to change but she wasn't quite sure what it was, or a quest for new ideas that she might incorporate into the worship at her church.

The second risk this pastor took was deciding to take some suggestions back to her congregation. She sketched a plan for improving the worship experience. She decided to improve her style, which meant she was stepping into new territories, learning new things. How well could she do a liturgy with which she had not been acquainted? Could she help the people in the congregation feel the same thrill and hope she felt when she participated in the experience at the workshop? If she couldn't, would she be a failure? What would the people in the congregation think of her innovations?

The third risk was sharing the proposed plan, especially the sanctuary improvements, with the small group. She had to prepare her proposal well so they would begin to see the benefits she thought might accrue because of the changes. She risked her trust level and her reading of their willingness to follow her suggestions.

The fourth risk was getting feedback and allowing this group to mull over, discuss, share, and consider her plan for a week. She could have asked for an immediate decision which she felt she could control. Once the group left the room, however, her influence waned as they interpreted and analyzed the plan from their perspectives.

The fifth risk was listening, at the second meeting, to the feedback and being willing to accept the modification in the sanctuary the one lay leader had proposed. Was she willing to accept the modification even though it was better than her original idea? What would that do to her future leadership? She took the risk of accepting and supporting the modification. Her plan was no longer her plan! It had been changed.

The sixth risk was signing a letter to the congregation which had been written by another leader. Her input to the letter was slight. Even riskier, she put it in the bulletin. Controversy might erupt! There were plenty of persons, she had been told, who might torpedo the proposal.

The seventh risk was sharing with the congregation some of the modifications she was making in the worship experience and telling them why. Not only would she be bound by these new procedures but her credibility was at stake because she was giving them reasons for the changes. This was a new level of exchange between herself and the congregation.

The eighth risk was allowing persons other than herself to present the proposal.

All eight risks occurred because of an announcement for a workshop on worship. Risks are present in every opportunity for new learning presented to pastors and leaders in the church. Learning new things is a risky business.

Risk 2: Learning About Yourself

If you've ever taken a personality-type test or answered a skills-aptitude questionnaire, you know how intimidating such tests can be. The pages in front of you are full of statements you know will tell somebody things about you. Do you answer the questions, select the statements truthfully, or, since you have done so many of these self-test instruments, do you skew the responses to reflect someone other than yourself?

"What difference does it make if I'm right- or left-brained? What can I do about it anyway? I'm doing a good job no matter what some person who reads tests says."

"I don't take any of those personality or leadership tests anymore. They don't tell me anything I don't already know about myself. Anyway, what good are they?"

Instruments designed to reveal your leadership or managerial qualities are not tests. They are self-help guides revealing traits or leadership qualities in terms of areas of dominance and areas of weakness. Once the guides have been analyzed, it is up to you to decide how to strengthen areas of weakness and how to broaden areas of dominance.

If you use a set of instruments and discover that you are left-brain (rational) dominant, then you can begin to find ways to develop your right-brain (feeling) in the same way you might increase scores on aptitude and IQ tests. The first step is wanting to make the changes, the second step is creating a plan, and the third step is following the plan to its successful conclusion.

How risky is it to learn about yourself? Ask the "leader" who believes in surrounding himself with persons who believe exactly as he does, who must approve everything purchased, who is the featured soloist in the choir, who must approve every committee's deliberations, and who tolerates others' points of view by ignoring them. How risky would it be for this person to see this picture of himself? If he approved of the picture, should he be permitted to continue serving as leader of a group of people striving to grow in grace and love?

Your perception of reality about yourself inevitably is fraught with layers of emotion. The play of emotions within is like the mosaics seen through a kaleidoscope; they change and shift with each movement. Trying to capture the real person through all the images is difficult for anyone. That's the reason it is risky to try to learn about yourself.

As a leader, however, you must continue to try to come to grips with who you are in order to provide a model for other leaders and for followers. Being a model is precisely what a leader is supposed to do. Leading is modeling behavior through inspiration, direction, support, suggestion, and conflict resolution, among other things. As a leader in the church, you must be careful about the kind of behavior modeling you are about. It must be consistent with the purpose and message of the Christ.

"Know thyself," "follow me," "let others bury the dead" are admonitions about the risk of knowing yourself. We are shaping people's lives in the church. If we are unwilling to "take the mote" out of our eye, how can we legitimately lead others? How do we know about the mote in our eye? The best way to learn about yourself is to risk taking self-administered inventories and doing something constructive with the results. It sounds simple, but it is very risky.

Risk 3: Trusting Others

"Not only was she my spouse for thirty years, she was my best friend."

"I'd trust her with my newborn child."

"I will give you my inheritance because I know you will do constructive things with it."

Trust is earned. Like a dish, trust is never entirely fixable once it is broken. It is an investment one makes in another person. Such an investment requires emotion, time, energy, and support. It needs special attention during times of stress.

One of the enduring values of having a police officer as a personal friend is understanding the meaning of trust. An officer I knew a long time ago told me that he trusted no one on the streets. They were his acquaintances; he knew them as business persons, as neighbors, as residents, as perpetrators, as petty thieves, as colleagues. But he trusted his partner on the beat and his colleagues in the station house with his life. He lived in a world I did not know, but his distinctions between acquaintance, awareness, and trust have remained part of my experience.

This police officer was acquainted with a lot of people by name or by position or by circumstance. These people were generally good, although any one of them might have some distinguishing idiosyncrasy. They were the majority of people with whom he came in contact. They were dependable and habitual. He expected them to act in certain ways, and they usually did. He depended on their habits to not make trouble for him or them. He found them dependable, and in that sense they were trustworthy.

Another group of people, a smaller contingent of the community, was "on the edge." He was aware of their potential. These were the people who tried to be his friends or who shied away from any contact with him. He did not trust them at all. He was constantly aware of their presence even when they were not physically evident.

Those he trusted were people with whom he had worked as colleague, peer, and friend. They had earned, through times of trial and happiness, his respect and trust. They had been at his side when his wife was ill, when his father had died, when he needed to talk, when he faced critical times on the street. These were the people who had been "with him" and had given him support at his times of need.

A leader in the church has much the same three audiences. Most of the people are acquaintances. They are people with needs, hurts, and happiness.

They call for help at times of grief, to have children baptized, to request a visit for a friend, to seek a prayer for themselves or a family member or a friend. They are the constituency that a pastor feels are dependable. They call and expect a response. They support the church by money and presence. They are dependable.

There is another group, smaller, who make themselves indelible on the consciousness of the church leader. They are either leading toward trouble in the organization or creating situations that cause a church leader to spend a great deal of time helping them. They have one crisis after another. Some of these crises actually are due to their relationship to the church.

The third group—those whom the leader trusts— is usually much smaller than need be. The most effective leaders in churches are continually striving to enlarge this group. The effective leader develops means for testing trustworthiness that are based on personal traits, rather than so-called religious traits like being at church whenever the doors open or reading the Bible from cover to cover every year. Trustworthy personal traits include dependability, sensitivity, reciprocal trust, understanding and support for the purpose of the church, and a life that seeks to mirror Christian ethical standards.

Many trustworthy persons exist in every church. It should not be difficult to find them, but the burden for seeking them rests with you as the leader. You might find it hard to say, "It's your job; you can do it without any interference from me." Trust, however, is a requisite in the church. After all, God has entrusted us with the message of love brought by Christ.

The more people you are able to bring into the circle of trust, the more opportunities for growth of the church, new leaders, and freshness among the current leaders of the church. Trust calls forth trust, creating a climate of mutuality. It is much better to have trust spread among many people than a few souls worn out by the stress of trying to "do it all" to keep the programs of the church moving forward.

Risk 4: Training Others

Perhaps your ultimate test as a leader is to train others to do jobs that you normally do. Think about the consequences of training others. They will take your jobs and leave you to do . . . what? You will have to develop new interests and skills. You will find yourself listening to their ideas and using some of them because they will be as good or better than yours. Training others is a risk indeed.

The pastor of a small congregation of about 150 members felt he was not being challenged enough. He needed to do something more but wasn't quite certain what it should be. If we were to analyze his situation we would call him underemployed.

This pastor liked to teach. He decided that there were two types of training he could do for which he was well prepared—teaching teachers and teaching persons to be potential preachers. He set a schedule of four meetings a quarter for nine months for potential teachers and the same number of meetings for potential preachers. He then invited six people for each of these courses. These people had to commit to twelve meetings over the nine months. The meetings were one and a half hours each.

At the end of the first year he had trained three teachers and two potential preachers. He had learned a great deal and now had five new leaders. The pastor and the five leaders continued the program the next year, expanding it so that the two potential pastors became a team and the three educators were another team. Thus, with the pastor, there were now three sets of courses, all the same, for other potential leaders.

During the second year, the pastor involved the two persons he had trained in designing and leading worship. The church school added a couple of classes including an adult course. The church began to become exciting. The number of people attending worship and church school started to increase, and the pastor found he didn't have as much time to put into teaching as he had had the previous year.

The third year the pastor decided to give the actual teaching over to the lay people. His tasks were more in the area of helping find potential students, helping create resources, and finding ways in which the graduates of these courses could use their newfound skills.

Over the years the little church became a very strong multi-thousand-member congregation. The attendance at the service is nearly 80 percent of the membership. Involvement is a key characteristic of the congregation.

This church is strong because the pastor took a series of risks to train people. A church becomes strong because a leader is willing to risk letting others into the circle of leadership, to train them, to give them resources, and to find appropriate avenues for the expression of their commitment.

Risks are stressful. Leading is stress ridden. Church leaders become more effective as they learn new things, continually try to better understand themselves, expand their trust base among the members, and train others. No leader approaches any of these risks without a sense of uncertainty and some trepidation.

CHAPTER FIVE

When It Is Appropriate to Be a Leader

I'm getting burned out! I think it's because I try to be all things to all people. I can't continue to be the Head of Everything!"

You don't need to take on all jobs in order to be a leader. Many tasks can be done by others so you can become a follower much of the time. This relieves your stress and helps develop other leaders. Sometimes it is appropriate to be a leader and, as we have seen, at other times it is more beneficial to be a Doer, a Talker, a Problem Solver, or any other of the myriad roles needed to make a church effective.

Various Roles Leaders Play

How do I lead? Let me count the ways. A paraphrase of an Elizabeth Barrett Browning poem suggests that leaders are multifaceted persons. They do not instigate everything that happens.

Winston Churchill, a model leader, led when it was important, supported when necessary, cajoled as needed, and inspired at critical times. His life pattern shifted back and forth between leader and follower, out front person, behind-the-scenes strategist, loyal subject, and outspoken critic. He is hard to put into a single category of human endeavor. He personified an effective leader.

An effective leader helps the church focus by regularly reminding the people of its vision and purpose, raising inspiring flags at particular moments of need.

A leader is supportive. A staff member of a church organization lost a spouse. Her boss, a leader in addition to being a boss, came to the home to express support and to share in the grief. The boss then had to leave on an assignment some distance away. Once at the new location the boss called to check on the staff member and to assure her that support was available.

A leader is a cheerleader. A church member was asked to become the head usher. His tasks included training ushers when to seat people; how to greet visitors; and how to conduct themselves during special services such as baptisms, communion, and funerals. He also recruited other persons to be ushers. During one of the training sessions, the new head usher was criticized for instructing other ushers to treat visitors with special care. The critical person, an usher and church member of some years, felt church members should be treated better than visitors. The new head usher went to the pastor, who complimented the head usher for the job being done, supported the need for treating visitors well, and encouraged him to continue the good work. The pastor acted as a leader, a cheerleader for the head usher.

A leader is an optimistic realist. A young woman pastor was assigned to an old city church. The building needed much repair, the average age of the congregation was over sixty years, the attendance was about forty on an average morning, and the feeling of those who were acquainted with the church was that it was either dead or dying.

The young woman knew the setting and, after studying the church's recent history, conceded that it had many problems. She also felt it had a future because of its people and the needs in the neighborhood. She instituted a process of renewal based on spiritual development and outreach. Within 18 months the church building had been refurbished, the average attendance at worship was 111, and the congregation included several young families with children. This young woman was realistic in that she understood the situation, but she was also optimistic because she saw possibilities. With her optimistic realism, she was able to lead the congregation into a new life of service.

A leader is sensitive. The pastor-parish relations committee had been meeting monthly for the past quarter because of complaints about the pastor's apparent unwillingness to visit people in hospitals and nursing homes. The committee chairperson was charged with informing the minister of the discontent within the congregation.

At their meeting, the pastor told the committee chair that he felt guilty about the situation. He couldn't bring himself to make those visits because of an experience he had had three months earlier. A young child had been seriously injured in an automobile accident and had died within three days. The pastor had visited the child and his family at the hospital each day until the death. He had been almost as devastated as the mother and father when the boy died. Since that time, the pastor had not been able to go back into a hospital without breaking down.

The committee chair sympathized with the pastor and assured him of support. Then, from the pastor's office with the pastor present, the chairperson called a grief counselor to make an appointment for the pastor. The chairperson told the pastor she would accompany him to the appointment but that no one else in the congregation would know about the situation.

She reported to the committee that the pastor was aware of the problem and would be back to visiting within a short time. Within two months, the pastor was able to resume visitation, and no one was the wiser. The chairperson was sensitive to both the pastor and the committee.

An effective leader plays many important roles other than being a manager or an administrator. Models of effective leaders often do not include characteristic care and concern people have for each other within a religious organization. This is a key difference between the roles of leaders in religious and nonreligious organizations.

Knowing When to Shift Roles

Driver training is conducted in most places using an automobile with an automatic transmission. This relieves the driver of the need to know when to shift gears, because the computer that controls the transmission makes those decisions. A driver who wants to control the shifting herself will purchase a car with a manual transmission, which allows her to control the gearing up or down based on her desires as to speed and traction.

An effective leader is a cross between these two types of transmission. Some responses are automatic: having ideas, identifying with the purpose of the organization, and talking. These are the external, visible signs of leadership. Few, if any, followers would be willing to be led by an individual without them. Other responses must be tailored to the situation.

Leaders must learn when to shift roles because, like a faulty transmission, they sometimes get stuck in the wrong mode.

In a crucial game, a referee called a foul on a player. The coach bowed his head but said nothing to the referee or anyone else at that time. At the next time-out, the player was blasted by the coach for making such a stupid mistake. After the game, an assistant coach asked the coach why it was necessary for the boy to be subjected to such severe abuse in front of players and spectators. The coach replied, "He deserved it."

The coach had not shifted from the mode of the authoritarian figure needed in coaching to that of a more humane person when he reprimanded the guilty player. Nor had he changed his role when the assistant spoke with him. He was stuck in automatic—winning was the need, the player's feelings were irrelevant.

Leaders in church organizations sometimes get stuck in automatic—a pastor on preaching or talking, a treasurer on costs and shortfalls, a lay leader on lack of participation, and so forth. It takes effort to shift from an accustomed and expected role to one that is supportive, creative, and optimistic.

Members of a congregation were discussing the need for a new program for adults in their late forties and early fifties whose children were leaving home. The pastor decided that she would be a listener, supporter, and problem solver rather than "preach" during program planning sessions. Her children were small, and she did not share the emotions of parents experiencing an empty nest. Nevertheless, the committee asked, "What do you want us to do?" The pastor told the members of the planning committee that *they* must decide if there was a need in the church and the community, what types of events or programs such persons might want, and the potential number of persons who might come to a series of programs. The pastor had to shift from an expected role of offering her ideas to one of listening. The shift was hard and had to be done *intentionally.*

If you are to be intentional in such a situation, you must *know when to change roles.* Careful observation and sensing the mood of a committee or group can help. Be attentive to indicators of when to change roles; they can slip by unnoticed. Watch the body language of members of the group. You might notice an involuntary shift of weight by a questioner who expects to be admonished or ridiculed for a "dumb" question, a whispered conference between two persons, a yawn or a glance at a watch. Be aware that such signs can indicate the need for you to change roles.

Being sensitive to shifts in moods, understanding that the Talker is trying to take control of a situation, allowing the Problem Solver to work magic in a hopeless setting are ways you can shift gears. It is usually up to you as a leader to make the shift. Invite intervention by someone else, then legitimate that person's contribution by words of support. Such invited intervention has saved many a meeting, and it can work for you!

Changing roles is risky because the meeting might move in a direction other than what you want. Be prepared for this; often the new direction will be a better one.

Being sensitive is a learned attribute for most of us, and good leaders practice it regularly. Leaders need to increase their aptitude for reading body language, hone their ability to sense the feel of a meeting, and learn when to back away from a posture that might suggest domination or intimidation.

How do you practice sensitivity? One way is to ask for assistance from people whose company you don't much care for but who can help a committee or group develop a workable program. Another way is to intentionally step out of your leadership role to let the committee or group select a different leader for a particular situation.

Sensitivity is gained with a cost. You will make a few mistakes—calling on the wrong person, stepping back too early or too late, or displaying insensitivity at the precise moment you are attempting to be sensitive. You will experience some embarrassment. You will learn to live with mistakes, and you will become more sensitive in the process. The effort to intentionally change roles will strengthen your long-term leadership.

Decision Making

"He's been threatening to bring the subject of two services to the committee for four months, but it isn't on this month's agenda either. Somebody needs to make a decision so that we know the direction to move in the Worship Committee."

"I think he's trying to get input from a variety of sources, including the feelings of the pastor."

"How many feelings does he need? We've had a survey of the members and attendees, met with the choir leaders and the organist, and we've developed several possible schedules that won't affect the church school's normal program."

Decision making is a critical part of leadership. In this case, the chairperson of the worship committee was forestalling a change by not deciding when to put an item on an agenda. Perhaps the chairperson himself didn't want more services than are now offered, but the number of services is not his decision to make. His decision—when to discuss an item—is as critical as deciding on the outcome of the item.

A leader's decisions are necessary and momentous. Of course, only a few decisions will immediately change the life and work of the organization; most will be felt by a few people and will initiate change gradually. For instance, deciding to institute training in the areas of preaching and teaching had a dramatic effect on the 150-member congregation described earlier. The decision was not momentous at the beginning for most of the members since only six people were affected. Yet, this little decision of a minister who was underemployed resulted in a vastly different congregation over time.

Many decisions go unnoticed at the time but are critical to the overall life and health of the church. The decision of the young woman pastor who accepted the challenge of a dying city congregation was a typical, if somewhat unusual, decision by a leader. She knew there would be consequences to the decision and had no idea where those new avenues would lead. She made a decision to accept this church as her responsibility.

Careers are set, partners selected, children conceived, and life courses determined by small, seemingly unimportant decisions. These "unimportant" decisions add up to important decisions. An effective leader thinks through all decisions and then makes them. A leader who is not effective makes judgments without considering possible outcomes or prefers to let situations dictate decisions.

Dealing with Conflict

"Do I have to like you in order to be a part of the leadership team?"

"No. You don't have to like me and I don't have to like you in order for us to work together. We can combine our expertise and experience to make this program work. Our personal feelings must be put to one side. I respect your abilities in this arena, and that is the most important ingredient I can bring to our common task."

A lay leader was recruiting a small group to design and conduct a financial campaign. The goal was to secure funding for a building that would replace the hundred-year-old facility the church had inherited from a congregation that had ceased to exist. These two persons had had a history of conflict between them, yet they were to be on the same committee.

The chairperson knew it was essential to have her long-time combatant on the committee because of that person's ties in the community and her experience as a fund-raiser. The chairperson knew also that she had to put aside her personal feelings in order to conduct a successful fund-raising campaign. She was prepared to handle the possible disputes in the committee by deferring to her opposite's expertise.

Conflict comes in all sizes and from unexpected sources. Choir directors choose children to sing and face reprisals from parents of other children. An innocent remark is construed as an attack by a person who is undergoing a trauma at this time. Greeting a friend in a group with "How are you feeling today?" may be interpreted by the recipient as an invasion of privacy if only the greeter knew the person had been ill.

Conflict is not always a test of wills or based on holding to a principle. Conflict can occur when a leader least expects or is prepared to deal with it. In this sense, a leader must be prepared at all times to handle conflict. It is never appropriate for a leader to be flippant, irreverent, disrespectful, or inattentive.

Effective leaders are sensitive to other people's feelings and positions in life. They respect the privacy of personal conversations and never reveal privileged information. Good leaders try to prevent as much conflict as possible by not creating situations in which conflict can be ignited.

The best method for handling conflict is to prevent it. Make certain your words; your body language; and the preparation for any meeting, presentation, or conversation are sensitive to, and supportive of, others. This is not to say that you must back down from a position when you feel strongly.

A couple went to see a guidance counselor and her supervisor about the manner in which the counselor was dealing with—*not* dealing with—their child. The conversation was pointed, but the parents were clearly supportive of the need for counselors and the difficult roles they play. As the conference was ending, the guidance counselor's supervisor said, "I take it then that Ms. Jude continues to be acceptable as the counselor to your daughter." The parents' response was, "No. That's not what is acceptable. Ms. Jude has displayed no sensitivity toward nor given any assistance to our daughter. She has done a terrible job of relating to our daughter, and we want a different counselor. Ms. Jude may be acceptable to others, but she is not acceptable as a counselor to our daughter."

The effort of the parents to be supportive and respectful had not conveyed their desire to have Ms. Jude replaced. They had to become more explicit.

Leaders find themselves in similar situations many times and are as surprised as these parents to learn that others perceive exactly the opposite of their intentions. In spite of the surprise, leaders must be prepared to restate their position so there is no ambiguity about it. Clarifying the situation is a good way to avoid misunderstandings, misperceptions, and conflict.

If you find it difficult to handle conflict, you might need some training in conflict resolution, management, and prevention. It will be worth your time; you will be able to use the techniques you learn in many and varied situations in the future.

CHAPTER SIX

Enabling Growth in Others and Yourself

Becoming more adept in leadership skills is not the same as learning a language or practicing motor skills. Growth in leadership occurs as you stretch into unknown arenas of endeavor. Forming good habits and a great deal of repetition help children grow in their skills. Habits and repetition may be detrimental to a leader's growth.

Leaders need to keep learning new ways to think, to plan, to be more sensitive, and to be trustworthy. For a good leader, growth must be constant. The assumption that leadership skills can always be improved creates an atmosphere within an organization that encourages leaders to grow.

Creating the Atmosphere

A music teacher prepared her elementary school-children to watch an abbreviated performance of the

Nutcracker ballet. She taught the first graders about a couple of short segments and asked them to pay careful attention and listen for the music so they could put the story in its proper context. She did the same for the second graders. The third graders had slightly longer segments to learn and anticipate, as did the fourth and fifth graders. They were prepared for the ballet.

At the performance, the audience was quiet and expectant, quite unlike other full-school assemblies. When the performance ended, the students remained quietly sitting even after the principal had completed his thanks to the performers and the students. He had to tell them they were excused.

The music teacher created the atmosphere for learning and experiencing the ballet. There was no loud shouting of "Pay attention" or "Sit down." The students had an investment in what was being presented because the teacher had prepared them. She did not go to any extremes; she simply did her job— she taught children music.

Leaders who do their jobs help others invest in doing their own tasks well. By their example and conscious decisions about what will best help others grow, good leaders will create an atmosphere of learning and growth.

Note one other thing about the teacher. She gave the students parts to learn that fit their learning curves and capacities. A good leader knows the learning curves, aptitudes, and interests of others. This takes time, but leaders must be able to decide how to put talents and abilities to best use.

Identifying Needs

Books of lists are quite popular these days. One of the more interesting sets of lists relates to getting ready for a wedding. Some of these wedding lists deal with minutiae, but all of them include needs of the bride and groom and the setting for the wedding. Many of them mention parents. While most parents feel they do not need a list, referring to those lists helps them remember details they might otherwise forget.

Lists help leaders remember the kinds of skills or components of jobs other leaders must have. For example, a treasurer ought to be able to deal with numbers. List making helps leaders better understand their jobs. It also assists them in knowing what kind of training they need to offer to those who work with them.

Many of us don't like lists. Somehow these "things to do" or "needs" are like a haunting message of what hasn't been done. But lists are essential, especially when it comes to deciding which of your natural leaders would most benefit from particular kinds of growth opportunities.

If you have a problem with making lists of skills or training needed in order to do a specific kind of job in your organization, remember how careful you are to make a list when your car needs attention or you have many errands to run. The list I take with me to the mechanic often is very detailed. Not only that, I sometimes interrupt my day to make certain the mechanic is acting on every one of the items on the list.

If we treat an automobile with such care, should we not be very careful to identify needs within the persons who share leadership with us? Good leaders use lists to help identify needs for the training and growth of others.

Selecting Appropriate Training

In the first French class I took as a freshman in college was a senior who was a star lineman on the football team. He and the teacher were on a first-name basis; they had had several opportunities to know each other since the football player had repeated the class more than once. It seemed to me that he could have taken a course other than French, but the curriculum said we needed a foreign language and this one was as foreign as he could get. He perceived French as not helpful, as a chore, as a loss of time and money.

A major issue facing a leader is deciding which courses to take and which would be beneficial for each of those whom the leader wants to train or to be trained. Training should not be perceived as a chore or as a loss of time and money.

The first question to ask about training is whether the offering is practical for the organization's future. A workshop for teaching a new kindergarten curriculum is not appropriate for a chairperson of the worship committee. A training course for using a new computer module for church finances will be quite helpful to both a treasurer and a financial secretary in spite of the training they might have had in computer bookkeeping.

The second criterion is whether the training is appropriate to the task. An advanced workshop on teaching the Bible is too much for a person who is just beginning to teach adult Bible study classes. A workshop to update the word processing skills of a secretary who has been using the word processing program will be helpful.

The third criterion relates to how many persons can benefit from any given workshop or course. An introduction of a new curriculum may be needed by all members of the education committee and the teachers in the church school. This workshop would be even more helpful if it had general and then age-specific segments. Such a workshop would be more frustrating than helpful if the chairperson of the education committee were the only participant from a given church.

The fourth criterion is cost. Note that this is not the primary concern. Training costs money; the leader must make a determination about the expected benefits and results of the training and consider the church's ability to pay.

Acting

"Plan your work and work your plan" was a favorite slogan of a colleague many years ago. Two principles were evident: you need to outline your activities every day, and, once the outline is in place, you must act. For many of us, procrastination is a fact of life. But the leader in us must break the bonds of inaction and make things happen.

A pastor was in a church that was contemplating relocation. A business wanted the site of the current church building and offered a sizable amount of money for it. The church's board received the offer and then "thought about it" for six months. The business was disgusted with the inaction and gave the church an ultimatum: Decide within a month.

The pastor, who had been party to the trustees' lack of decision, felt it was time to act. He called a congregational meeting, and a vote was taken. The sale of the current property and relocation of the church passed by one vote. The pastor said the church had a mandate, and the church began negotiating with the business for the final sale.

A one-vote margin is hardly a mandate, but the pastor exercised a leader's need to act. He read the vote of the meeting and knew that many of those who voted against the move were persons who scarcely ever attended. The active, financially supportive members of the congregation were overwhelmingly in favor of the move. What did the pastor do so that he was able to call a one-vote margin a "mandate"?

This leader did several things to precipitate the decision. First, he called for a meeting at which a final vote was to be taken. Second, after that call for a meeting he sent a letter to all members outlining the rationale behind the proposed move. He included a map that showed where members currently lived and where population growth was expected because of housing developments. Third, he displayed the site plan and architectural drawings for the proposed new building. Fourth, he took the trustees as a group to the new site and walked them through the new building plan, drove them around the immediate area so they could see the extent of new housing being built, and arranged for them to spend half an hour with the developer of the new community. Fifth, the pastor called in a consultant to look at the current building and its program and the proposed site and its community. The consultant met with the trustees and board of the church to give them an expert opinion as to benefits and problems with the proposed relocation. Sixth, on the day of the vote, all members who came, including the inactives, had the right to vote. Seventh, when the vote was counted and a one-vote margin was evident, he proposed that the church develop a mission program for the current community so that those who were in the area would continue to be served by this church.

This leader's actions were a series of coordinated movements, not a solitary call for a meeting. Leaders learn to act on several fronts at the same time in order to ensure positive results.

The same attention to detail is required in decisions relating to training. Scheduling a person's attendance at a training event must be accompanied by making certain the fee is paid, arranging for the person's transportation to and from the event, securing the materials needed, and providing opportunities for applying what is learned from the training. This last item may be the most difficult to follow through on, since training will propose changes in the way things are being perceived and done.

An executive in a small business sent the foreman and three production team leaders to a workshop on building and strengthening teams in the workplace. The four people returned full of energy and excitement. In their meeting with the executive, these four people made several proposals for improving their production process. The proposals entailed some expenses in moving equipment and the purchase of a new machine that the executive had not counted on.

At the meeting the executive realized that to deny the implementation of changes would be to counter the training. He suggested the four continue to work with him to create a plan of implementation that would include the purchase of the new equipment.

Within two weeks the plan was in place. The executive then empowered these four people to implement the changes they had proposed in their work teams and make the changes necessary in the workplace.

The executive, as a leader, had chosen the people for training and had selected the training appropriate for their situation. He had not counted on what happened next. In order to be consistent with the goals of empowerment and improvement in production, the executive had to act on several fronts. He had to help these four trainees put into action some of their new ideas. He had to allocate funds. In addition he also had to interpret these actions to the remaining members of the work force as an experiment in increasing productivity.

Training will produce unexpected results. Leaders who insist on getting people trained must be willing to follow through on the proposals these trainees will bring from their workshops. It is most helpful if the trainees work with the leader in deciding which of the ideas might work best in which sequence so that the enthusiasm from the training is channeled into program areas with the most potential.

Growth occurs in us and in others as we learn new habits. This is one of the most difficult of all aspects of leadership because it makes us change. Those of us who begin a regimen of exercise after having been sedate for some time know the aches of muscles that haven't worked hard for a while. This same principle is at work in leaders who are changing. Keeping your purpose before you will help you deal with the "aches and pains" that can accompany change.

CHAPTER SEVEN

Testing Yourself as a Leader

A coach with more losses than wins is not a leader. A pastor with a declining membership and attendance record in a congregation is not a leader. A boss of a company that goes bankrupt is not a leader.

You might well say that these generalizations are inaccurate and unfair. But they point out that people evaluate on the basis of evidence they can see and measure. Whether we care to acknowledge it or not, people continually evaluate our leadership.

Feedback Process

A former mayor of New York often asked, "How'm I doin'?" This question usually was asked about a specific incident or speech or ruling he had made, not his overall job as leader of the city. It was his way of getting people to give him immediate feedback. The questioning often opened the door for people who were disaffected to let the mayor have a glimpse of a side of an issue he may not have known about.

An effective leader finds ways to hear the other side. This is more difficult than it seems. A consultant was meeting with a committee whose responsibility it was to have regular sessions with a bishop to exchange information about how things were going in the area. The committee chairperson said their meetings with the bishop consisted of the bishop's telling them what she was doing and why. After the bishop left, the committee proceeded to discuss the situation in the area and wonder why the bishop didn't know how bad things really were.

The consultant asked the committee chairperson if the committee included the bishop in their discussions. "No. Why would we do that?" The committee responsible for giving feedback to the bishop did not consider it their responsibility to provide the bishop the reality tests she needed in order to be an adequate leader.

It is essential to have an established and formal feedback process so people who need to know hear what is really being said about the organization and its leadership. When the formal feedback system doesn't work, new mechanisms must be established.

Tom Peters, a business consultant of renown, advocates that leaders walk through their businesses regularly at unexpected times. This allows the leaders to observe and hear what is happening at the work stations where customers are being heard and served.

The executives at Walt Disney World are required to spend an hour each day walking through the theme park to observe and listen to customers and employees. Then the executives proceed to their underground offices. They have participated in an informal "on-site feedback process."

The issue for both Tom Peters and Walt Disney World is hearing and seeing what is happening in the organization and in its relationship with the world. Changes in operations are made on the basis of such feedback, although more formal tests are usually conducted prior to substantial change.

Leaders need to know what other leaders are thinking, what policies are doing to the morale of employees and volunteers, what effect programs are having on people, and the kinds of people being attracted by the programs. None of these pieces of information may be immediately apparent to a leader who does not circulate among people and visit programs.

For instance, it is very difficult for a pastor or church school principal or superintendent to know what is happening in church school classes when she is teaching in the church school and has no regular program of "drop-in" visits to classes of all ages. Without such on-site visits it is difficult to schedule appropriate and regular training for church school teachers and leaders. Leadership includes serious concern and visible direction of growth programs for people, whether these be volunteers, staff members, participants in church programs, or a group or committee which you head. Leadership requires constant visitation and listening—ongoing feedback and learning.

Tests

As we saw in chapter 4, you can take any one of several types of self-administered leadership inventories in order to test your inclinations as a leader. These inventories indicate leadership qualities that you are likely to display under conditions outlined in the statements or questions. You should view these inventories as *indicators* rather than as final verdicts of your leadership capabilities.

"I just took the ——— inventory and discovered I am not as rational as I thought I was." This leader went on to say that, on looking back on her decisions, she had displayed this inclination at several important points over the past year. She was depressed.

It is important to remember that the inventory is a measure of current strength, not of ultimate leadership direction. This leader could well have said, "I have decided, on the basis of this inventory, to focus on learning planning skills and rational decision-making techniques. In fact, I have enrolled in a workshop next month to start me in that direction." An inventory is a statement of where a leader is at the present, not where the leader should be within the next months or years.

Evaluating Performances

The memo said, "It's time for your annual performance interview. Please complete the following form as a basis for the meeting." The form had several questions about likes and dislikes about the job and goals for next year. Not much was on the form to help the person do a self-evaluation.

Membership and attendance are indicators of performance for pastors. When both fall over a year or two, serious questions about performance need to be answered. Some of these questions may not be easy to answer, and most will have unflattering responses. However, the evaluations should provide a basis for change of direction both for the pastor and the church experiencing the declines.

Income and sales are better indicators of business performance than is net profit. Net profit is affected by decisions about expenditures that may or may not be helpful to the health of the business. But increasing sales and income indicate that the business is on the right track.

You will be a more effective leader if your performance is evaluated regularly. Ideally, you should be evaluated by everyone affected by your leadership decisions and actions. The loop for getting the evaluations back to you is the feedback process.

Two kinds of evaluations are essential for leaders. The first is formal evaluation, and the second is informal evaluation.

No doubt you have seen workshop leaders give out an evaluation form to every participant at the beginning of a session. The completed forms are read carefully by the leaders following the workshops in order to better understand how they are being received and how well the messages they are giving are getting through. This short questionnaire is a formal evaluation instrument.

Informal evaluations can be more difficult to secure. Golf games, bowling parties, coffee meetings with friends and associates provide opportunities for talking about leadership style and decisions. Anyone who has had a difficult message to express to a leader about style knows that there is no good time in which to do it. No one likes to hear how she or he needs to improve or how badly she or he blew the last decision.

One of my colleagues asked an associate to evaluate a paper she had written. The associate read the paper and made notes at various points. He thought she truly wanted a stronger paper. He gave it back to her and she refused to talk to him for a month. Finally she told him that he had been so insensitive with his comments that she had cried from humiliation upon reading his notes.

Leadership functions are so much an expression of ego that any criticism or comments about your leadership can be construed as an attack on you personally. Once when I was batting I was hit on the arm by a fastball. It took the welt nearly a week to go away. That was a speedy recovery compared to the time it would take me to recover from a person's comments about how poorly I led a meeting. The difference is that my body heals automatically, but my psyche needs specific attention to separate my skills from my ego.

If you are giving feedback to another leader, be as supportive as possible. There are diplomatic ways of saying one needs improvement: "You did a nice job in this situation. I wonder if making a suggestion that the person look at it another way might have helped him better understand your reason for making the decision?"

Do not be fooled into thinking that private conversations are invitations to make personal attacks on other leaders. They are human and have emotions, just like you. Think of how you might respond before being too blunt in an evaluation. And you will be better able to notice when people are giving constructive criticism to you.

CHAPTER EIGHT

Getting Honest Feedback

You think I'd tell him how he comes across? I like what I do too much to be that foolish!"

"But he says he wants feedback. Isn't that feedback?"

"Yeah. But he doesn't want to hear honesty. He wants sugar-coated criticism, and only a little of that, and a lot of ego strokes."

"Isn't he a leader? I thought they were supposed to be able to deal with criticism."

"He's a leader all right. I don't think he knows anything about dealing with criticism and making changes."

Whether or not this leader wanted honest feedback, he is not about to get it from these volunteers. They are content to "wait him out" because his term will be over before they want to quit doing their church tasks.

Some leaders go for years without getting a single item of honest feedback. When they finally hear honest evaluation, they are devastated because they have been led to believe they are doing a good job. Honest feedback is critical to leaders because it is necessary if they are going to grow.

Honest feedback can be gotten only if a leader has displayed personal integrity, approachability, and an ability to listen and change.

Personal Integrity

A young woman worked in a department store and was embarrassed by a manager who came over occasionally. This manager made disparaging comments about and to the young woman in front of customers. After such a session one day, the young woman told the manager that it wasn't right for her to embarrass an employee in front of customers; if she had something to criticize, it would be fine to do so after the customers had gone or if she took her to one side. The manager fired the young woman.

Integrity, being able to confront a picture of oneself held by someone else, is critical to a leader. Being honest with yourself and with others is part of integrity. Having a morality that enables you to treat others as yourself is another part of integrity. The manager did not display any of these characteristics. She was not a leader. She could not take honest feedback.

Some leaders in the church display, intentionally or unintentionally, the same kind of spirit the manager showed. They are not comfortable with volunteers who disagree with them theologically or in any other way. They are unwilling to accept even the slightest nuance of criticism. They must be the stars of the show no matter the setting. Such leaders neither personify the gospel nor display integrity. Unless they are willing to take some risks, they will continue to be poor leaders.

Approachability

Two women were discussing their boss's gruff exterior as they ate lunch. They agreed that he was really a cream puff on the inside, but getting to him meant braving the rough exterior. They thought any efforts they made would be put off. They decided it wasn't worth the effort to find a good way to approach him to suggest changes in one part of his style.

People usually observe a leader for a while before deciding on the leader's approachability. No matter what a leader says, people wait to see what happens when one or two brave souls make the initial approach. Then they assess whether or not the leader can be talked to about certain topics.

A congregational leader told the congregation he would be available for informal conversations for three hours two mornings each week. He invited them to drop in or to telephone during these hours. If what a member needed to say to him took more than five minutes, he and the member would schedule another time for further discussion.

A woman decided this would be a good time to see if there was an opening for her to train for some church work she had been considering. Her call was answered by the leader, who paid scant attention to what she said and had to ask her name twice. He told her he would call back within a day, but two weeks later she had not heard from him. As she told her story, which was repeated with various emendations throughout the congregation, the number of calls and visitors for informal conversations got fewer and fewer. Within a month the leader decided no one wanted to take advantage of this opportunity and canceled the program.

This leader had demonstrated that he was not approachable no matter what he had said. One woman's experience was enough to convince the congregation that what the leader said and did were inconsistent. He never understood that he was the culprit who shot down his own program.

Words and invitations are important, but behavior makes or breaks a leader. It is wise to remember that approachability is demonstrated, not discussed or described or scheduled.

An Ability to Listen and Change

"Talk is cheap" is a phrase leaders must take to heart. Actions are the critical factor in leadership.

"Mommy, I'll never do that again if you let me stay up for the next special on television."

"You have to go to bed because you broke the rules we had agreed on. Perhaps you can think about what you did and figure out how not to do it again while you are in your bed."

Whole sets of literature focus on the need to do rather than discuss doing. The message of this literature, much of it from folk tales, should be taken to heart by leaders. Agreements, speeches, private encouragement are useless unless there is a demonstration that the leader is truly willing to listen and to change.

The encounter of Jesus with a rich man (Matthew 19:16-24) is a prime illustration of our willingness to commit in words but not to put our life into alignment with our speech. The rich man wanted to be a disciple of Jesus, but he didn't want to give up his other god—money and possessions.

A pastoral relations committee met with a pastor and gave him a list of specific changes the congregation was demanding of him. The pastor agreed to make the changes—visiting more, attending meetings, and helping to develop programs. At the three-months' review of his actions, the committee decided nothing had changed. They were outraged that this pastor, by his actions, considered them nothing more than troublemakers. With the support of the congregation, they suspended the pastor immediately and refused to allow him into the church any more.

Demonstrating the ability to listen and change is critical for a leader who intends to lead.

A positive response to honest feedback is a gift reserved for those few leaders who show personal integrity, whose demeanor makes them approachable for any topic, and who have demonstrated the ability to listen and learn. If you wish to be an effective leader, you will need to practice these attributes until you earn the privilege of receiving honest feedback.

CHAPTER NINE

Leading in a Change Process

Eight out of ten people have problems making changes. The degree of resistance to change varies from "I'm not going to" at one extreme to "Convince me of the value" at the other end of the spectrum. Of course there is another group who wants to change because they crave excitement and challenge. Leaders must cope with the 80 percent while reining in the 20 percent.

Using Different Words

Bob didn't like any change. He complained when a new typeface was used for the bulletin; he criticized the pastor for adding a prayer time in the service; he fought as a member of the board to return to one service. Bob's world was structured, and he wanted to keep it neat.

Professionally, Bob was a salesman whose line of products kept changing. He never complained about these changes. When he was asked about his aversion to change and the continued changes in the products he sold, Bob replied, "The products I sell do not change. They are improved and made easier to use. The products changed from steel to plastic components because they were lighter and wear just as well. We don't *change*. The customers wouldn't buy if we did. They buy because we *improve*."

Change, like radical surgery, is a matter of perspective. For many people any surgery is radical—much like Bob's perception of change. Leaders who are effective know many people like Bob. These leaders know that to use the word *change* is to invoke major resistance. However, to discuss "improvement" is a move in the right direction.

Words are critical when discussing change. *Growth* is a bad word for some people, but "taking care of young families with babies" propels the same people into action to improve the nursery. After all, this nursery might be needed when the grandchildren visit or when the niece with her small children moves to town. The fact that an improved nursery can assist in growth is irrelevant to getting the project under way.

Fixing the lighting and repairing the stairs are not changes. Granddad needs to see so he can sing, and Uncle Mort needs a rail to lean on as he uses the stairs. If someone said, "We need to change the lighting and fix the stairs," an outcry about cost would drown out those bent on making the repairs. When change is put into terms of aiding people who have known needs, the adjustments are no longer changes. They become necessities.

Improving the interior means painting the dull gray walls an off-white. *Enhancing the sound of the organ* means getting a major overhaul. *Adjusting the time of the service* to accommodate those who get up early means adding a second service. *Strengthening the program* means adding an additional staff member. The words do not say "change," even though that is exactly what is planned. *Change* is a flag word that effective leaders should use cautiously, if ever. Change is fine, but use different words to describe what is happening!

Preparing the Groundwork

A woman pastor was assigned to a city church that had a long heritage. This church was across the street from a major transit stop where thousands of people each day caught the bus or train to the downtown sections of the city. The building was about a hundred years old and contained the pastor's living quarters. When the pastor went to the church it had nine members with an average attendance of about twelve.

You might believe that the situation was so bad when the pastor went to the church she could have suggested anything and the members would have done it. Not true. These nine members had been with the church during its years as a strong witness in the area and had had exceptional pastors. They stayed on despite the decline in membership. They had not been willing to change. They were stuck in the past.

The pastor looked at the area, identified the groups the church could reach, and decided on a plan of action. In the meantime, she visited the members in their homes and got to know each one of them. During these visits she asked them the best things about the church and what they wished for. The responses varied, but the main theme of the members was a strong church with a community outreach.

The pastor told the congregation at the first worship service that she liked to have music and would find and invite some people to sing and play during most worship services. She went to a nearby laundromat and put up a note asking for instrumentalists who would be willing to volunteer to play at a worship service. Within a month, she had interviewed and listened to several potential instrumentalists. She selected and invited a trumpeter, a clarinetist, a drummer, and a French horn player to come together for practice to play at one or two services. In addition, she asked three violinists, a viola player, and a bass player to practice for two or three services.

An audience of nine is not much of an incentive for musicians so one morning the pastor asked the worshipers to help her by suggesting ways to fill the sanctuary for these musicians who were giving of their time and talent. The nine members sat silent for a few minutes and then said, "We don't know how to do that."

It was at this meeting that the pastor told the members what she had heard them say about their church and what they hoped for it. She suggested that the best thing for them to do was to close out the old church with its glorious history and start a new church where they didn't have to drag around all of their yesterdays as they planned for tomorrow. Silence. "Now maybe that wouldn't be such a bad idea." The leader of the members had given his approval!

The pastor had prepared carefully. She had listened to the members. She had visited them in their own surroundings. She knew their hopes. She had asked about music because several of them had said how nice it had been when there was an orchestra and a brass quintet in the worship services. She had looked at the neighborhood and assumed that many musicians, artists, and aspiring actors lived in the apartments around the church. She knew one of the common grounds of all these young people was the local laundromat. She had spoken with consultants about what to do with a church with a long history and no future so long as there were only nine members. She had made a plan. She decided what to do. She did it.

Three years later the congregation has a worship attendance of over 120 with a membership of 240. Growth continues. The old building has been refurbished and now is able to accommodate programs attractive to the people in the neighborhood. The nine members are the pastor's staunchest supporters.

Change doesn't just happen. In this instance, and in most places without a cataclysmic cause, changes are as carefully choreographed as a ballet. Preparation is critical. Without her careful preparation, this pastor would have been as successful as her predecessor, who saw a decline in the membership from seventy-five to nine.

Creating Step-by-Step Implementation

A District Superintendent had a Caucasian church in an area in which 90 percent of the population was African-American. The superintendent knew there was no future for the existing congregation. He also knew there needed to be a new church to minister to the majority of the community residents. He decided that the best method for getting the new church was to close out the Caucasian church and start a new African-American congregation using the same building.

His plan was to find a person who could be the pastor of a new African-American church. He visited a nearby seminary. The potential pastor was in his second year and would graduate in a year. The super-intendent asked him if he might consider an assign-ment to start a new church. The potential pastor told the superintendent it would be a year before he was ready and that he might need some help the first few months since he had never been a pastor before. The superintendent assured him that he would be with him during those months and would leave as soon as the new pastor demonstrated enough confidence to be the sole leader of the new church.

Step one had been accomplished: A pastor had been found for a new African-American congregation.

Step two was to work with the Caucasian congregation to make certain it would be willing to close and leave its building to the new church. The superintendent preached every third Sunday at this church during the summer and fall. He gained the confidence of the leadership of the church and began to discuss their future. He brought in data about the area and suggested the need for outreach into the community. They agreed to a plan of visitation and evangelism in the community.

Step three was to bring in the potential pastor as a community visitor and an intern pastor for six months to see if there was a chance the church could become attractive to the community. The experiment with the intern pastor was not successful because the church was considered by the neighborhood as a Caucasian church and the people wanted a church of their own heritage.

Step four of the plan was to suggest to the congregation that it consider closing. This was done three months prior to the actual timetable for bringing in a new pastor. The discussion about closing was based on their past accomplishments and the continuation of their outreach by leaving their building to allow ministry to continue in the community. After considerable discussion, the congregation voted to close out the church and let the superintendent use the building for a new African-American church to be established at the time of a new pastor's appointment.

Step five of the superintendent's plan was to make certain the building was in good condition. After the vote to close, the superintendent told the Caucasian congregation that its mission would be greatly enhanced if it would make certain repairs so the new congregation would not be burdened with debt in order to have a decent and usable church building. After considerable debate, the Caucasian congregation agreed and paid for the repairs.

Step six was to start the new church. At the appointed time, the Caucasian church held its last service in its building. The next week, the superintendent and the young African-American pastor held services for a handful of African-Americans who would be the nucleus of the new congregation. The new pastor, because he had been an intern for six months, had recruited these persons.

Within a month, the superintendent gave the total leadership over to the new pastor, which was step seven of his implementation plan. He continued to give support to the new pastor and watched the congregation increase to seventy. He also watched the new pastor implement several community-oriented programs aimed at getting young people off the streets. The new church and the new pastor were going to make it as a viable congregation.

Step eight of his plan had to be given over to his successor. This was to rebuild the old church building so that it would be usable for the kind of ministry needed and desired by the new church.

The superintendent had done his homework by learning about the church, examining its history, trying to understand the new community in which it was located, and making some decisions about the future of the church and its possible ministry. The superintendent had then developed a plan that included recruiting a pastor, helping the Caucasian congregation understand its best approach to ministry, and easing this congregation out while preparing the new pastor and the community for a new church. The components of the plan were worked out over a two- to three-year period.

Plans do not spring full-blown into one's head. An idea about the future desired result is developed. From this end result, an effective leader thinks through the steps necessary to get there. Once the various steps are put in proper order, a reasonable time schedule is established. This is a normal planning process. It doesn't start as a full-fledged plan, but as an end result that may be two or three years away. The step-by-step process is created based on the realities of the situation.

The process and the implementation schedule are critical for a leader who must then act to make certain something happens.

Being Patient—Again!

"Patience is a luxury I can't afford. I only have a short time to see if this area can support a new church."

In fact, the leader who said this died seven months later. His appointment of a pastor to the area proved to be a good one as the new church was started and grew.

What does patience mean in a change process? Patience must not be confused with procrastination. Putting off a decision or deciding not to do something because "the timing doesn't seem right" are illustrations of indecision which may have serious negative consequences.

A congregation saw an area to the east of it growing rapidly and asked the superintendent what was being done to start a new church. The reply was, "We're waiting to see what develops." The congregation decided to act. They employed an associate pastor with the stipulation that half his time would be devoted to establishing a new church in the growing area. If after five years that was impossible, they would call an end to the experiment and they would be no worse off.

The associate came, looked at the statistics for the area, and began visiting. Within a year, he determined that a new church should be started and recruited the aid of the District Superintendent in making the necessary arrangements for forming a new church. The new church was started, and after six months it had an average attendance of about two hundred. The sponsoring congregation allowed the associate pastor to go full time to the new church within two years. In order to be true to their five-year obligation the congregation donated enough money to purchase a parsonage for the new church.

In this illustration, the sponsoring congregation displayed patience. They were willing to give a pastor up to five years to decide whether a new church could be started and then to get it going. In this setting, the situation was such that it took less than two years for the new church to be on its own.

In a quite different setting, a new employee was brought into a busy, high-tech office. The new hire was willing to learn but brought little experience to the tasks. She did not respond to training immediately. The environment of the office was such that an investment had been made in this person, and she was to be given every opportunity to prove her capabilities. Her training continued, and the young woman became acclimated to the environment and the job. Within eighteen months, she was a strong member of the office team.

Patience is supported by action. There must be a reason to be patient—perhaps to allow an individual to acquire skills or for a leader to collect data and develop a plan.

Patience requires work on the leader's part. In the case of the young woman in the office, the leader had to help identify training courses that would give her confidence in herself as well as skills to do tasks. In the case of the congregation, it required the associate pastor to give monthly accounts of time and progress in starting a new church. In the case of the superintendent starting a new African-American congregation, it required him to be active on two fronts, with the potential pastor and with the existing congregation.

As a leader, you will find your patience wearing thin when you do little to support or direct those who depend on your leadership. You can measure the results of patience by how active you are behind the scenes during a time when incremental change is occurring. Remember that most change does not occur instantly but comes about because of a plan and hard work. When people believe nothing is happening, you should be busy in the background!

Counting Gains—Not Setbacks

"Guess what. Jenny took her first step today." This means the child took one step and fell down on the second. Did the mother mention the second step? No! She was interested in change, the baby's shift from being a crawler to a walker.

A young man was batting for only the twenty-fifth time in organized baseball. He had made twenty-four straight outs. This time he lined a single into center field. He stood on first base like a king. He had changed from an easy out to a hitter! The twenty-four previous outs had a new perspective.

An artist was surrounded by crumpled paper as she worked at the easel. She made a stroke and stood back to look for the umpteenth time. "I did it! Look at that nose!" She had gotten the nose right. She was successful. Now she could throw all those other noses away!

Change is measured by gains. You will always have setbacks, but they are put into perspective by the incremental gains. It is the gains—not the setbacks—that are important.

When a majority of persons are against change, you must expect many setbacks. All who try to make adjustments in the environment in which they work will be frustrated many more times than they are elated. But remember the elation; learn from the frustrations. That's the way progress is measured.

Leading in a change process is difficult but rewarding. It is made somewhat easier by knowing you are never leading by yourself. You have allies and supporters. At the same time, decisions and implementation are based on your preparation and patience. The rewards of such leadership are counted as progress "on my watch."

CONCLUSION

Each of us has leadership skills, although many of us try to hide them. We are all called upon to lead at one time or another. The fact that you have leadership skills does not mean you must lead at all times in every situation. Leadership skill includes knowing when to be in front and when to follow. Learning the latter may be the most difficult skill of all.

You will continue to hear calls for leadership. How you respond will depend greatly on your confidence as a person. God depends on people who acknowledge the calls and serve as effective leaders, always learning more about leadership and honing skills. The world will be a better place when effective leaders are willing to respond *as real leaders* at crucial times demanding their skills.